MAP TO THE STARS

MAP TO THE STARS

ADRIAN MATEJKA

PENGUIN POETS

PENGUIN BOOKS

An imprint of Penguin Random House LLC
375 Hudson Street
New York, New York 10014
penguin.com

LIBRARY OF CONGRESS CATALOGING-IN-PUBLICATION DATA
Names: Matejka, Adrian, 1971– author.
Title: Map to the stars / Adrian Matejka.
Description: New York, New York : Penguin Books, [2017] | Series: Penguin poets
Identifiers: LCCN 2016041453 (print) | LCCN 2016049078 (ebook) | ISBN
    9780143130574 (softcover) |
ISBN 9781524704148
Subjects: | BISAC: POETRY / American / African American. | POETRY / American
    / General.
Classification: LCC PS3613.A825 A6 2017 (print) | LCC PS3613.A825 (ebook) |
    DDC 811/.6—dc23
LC record available at https://lccn.loc.gov/2016041453

Printed in the United States of America
10 9 8 7 6 5 4 3 2 1

Set in Adobe Caslon Pro
Designed by Bonni Leon-Berman

For Natasha and Rik

who aren't named

but are part of every

"we" and "us" in these poems

CONTENTS

SOUNDS OF EARTH

STARS ALREADY

Why should you leave the stars
And the sun and the moon
And the universe all alone?
            —*Sun Ra*

Except that Strong Men are
Pasted to stars already.
            —*Gwendolyn Brooks*

Star-Struck Blacks

Again, winter & Indianapolis's 30th Street Bridge
is salty over the iced-up White River. & above

both salt & ice, stars constellate into back-lit animals
& ancient heroes posturing in the edges of the Earth's

afro—as inevitable as morning frost in morning
hair after a park bench sleep. & more syncopated

lights move on the horizon lowly the way cop lights
always move to wherever black people collect

outside of church. All this fast stereotyping
like the manicured fingers in the steno pool where

those same cops linger, badges shining & hats under
arms before testifying that they shot in self-defense.

Back at the bridge, two brothers are peeing into
the monochromatic current, backs graffitied by a great

migration of taillights. One brother stares North,
way up toward Saturn, & says, *Man, I bet this water*

is cold. The other brother gravitates in the same
unreachable direction & says, *Yeah, I bet it's deep, too.*

CONSTELLATIONS
AND OTHER MOTIVES

Final Frontier

—after Gwendolyn Brooks

Big eyes & impossible sleep over here east
of the bridges potholed like empty tempos
as the abandoned hubbub of rusty axles
on busted concrete echoes in every direction.
The wheeze & cough as the furnace starts up
would sound less like an extraterrestrial in the hall
closet if my homemade tent staked a backyard
instead of a drafty townhouse. If the tent
was made out of polyethylene instead of thrifty
towels. We have a brown couch, a dining table
with a trick leg & two chairs. A black & white set
with its own wheeled stand. A secondhand
turntable that works when we can find a good
needle. Curtains, too & behind them: my back
up against a metal chair leg & the exoskin
of towels between me, the slick-skinned Dracos
& Ursa Minors skulking around horizons
& after-school centers on after-school specials.
The neighbors' same-old same-old aggravates
the plaster & particle between our spaces.
They are counting ones & fives toward another
break up to make up. Being broke is what it is
& every smashed plate & hair-pulling yelp

flows around that slim fact to the nervous middle
of the week when meals get skeptical
in the hungry days before payday. Even when
they're not fighting, they are anxious & red-eyed
in unison, couched in front of the only projector TV
in the area: *Star Trek* reruns every Saturday
at 9pm. The neighbors zip themselves up in lined,
open-nosed motions at the exact same time
Voyager 2 takes pictures of Saturn's bluer
parts & my mother's exhaust sparks little suns
when she finally pulls up after working late
again. It's already 1981, but the neighbors
still sound like a star fumbling for its keys.

& Later,

one of the star-eyed neighbors
spills white all over

the carpet again & leans into

    it like sniffing
    a fish's ear.

The other neighbor
is Pisces reclining,

    So & So on the couch
    in Atari's glow.

All of these habits

    from Vietnam, blamed
on Agent Orange—

    heroin & gunplay
first, cocaine after.

Not every fatherless black could
object to war like Sun Ra did.

Not every fatherless black could
get kicked out of the army
        before the fighting

started like Richard Pryor.

Hardly any fatherless blacks
could skip Vietnam,

        as far out from this space
        as any black boy will get.

Listen: the neighbor's cigarette
        is about to burn into
        her own hair violently,
        the same way it burned

a socket into that unfortunate
shag rug in their living room.

Listen: we have to get
        off this pockmarked planet.

Read Between the Lines

213b opens brightly,
    like a newly discovered
planet on the front page

of a paper nobody reads
    & Garrett rolls out
of that revelatory linoleum,

left half of his afro as flat
    as the tire on his mother's
car back when she still

tried to drive us to school.
    Cheap snick of the door
locking behind him

like somebody trying out
    an empty lighter. Then, red
brick of cold air into

hot lungs. Carriage House
    East where menthols cough
the same octave as windows

slamming shut & outside
  those windows, somebody's
radio is already popping music.

The morning moon looks
  like part of a whole note.
That's when Garrett & I

down stroke to PS113, past
  triplicated sections of brick,
coupled rows of townhouses

facing each other like they
  are about to get into it.
Past snowdrifted dumpsters

& beneath those frozen
  silhouettes: spray-painted
tags & misspelled love

letters I couldn't decipher
  in the summer. Garrett
has been listening to Richard

Pryor again & says, *Fuck*
  those beat-ass muthafuckas
at school, Jack, & I agree,

too scared to disagree—
    walking past a mimeograph
of Mickey Mouse smiling

as he flips Iran the bird
    in the landlord's window.
We threw up the same

middle-finger salutation
    to the bus driver & he gave
it right back in a crescendo

of steering-wheel knuckles.
    So we ignored him & our bus
stop & kept walking Carriage

House–style—right hand
    skimming from chest
down to waist then behind

the back like a swimmer
    cupping water in a city
pool. Cue sirens snagging

morning air like hurtful
    afro picks. Cue the barking
of early-morning walks

to school in the snow.
    We forward leaned into
our strut like the disenchanted

streetlamps alternating
    between our side & the fenced
porches on the other, rotted

slats breaking like teeth
    right after the punch, right
where Garrett's cousin—

the one who stole on us
    every time we got close
to her—leaned into

the winter brick. She put
    two-fingered guns
to her temples when she saw

us, smoked-out patches
    of skin around her mouth
like a raw sun rising.

Post-Vietnam Blacks

There's the upward mouth of space—

the honeyed smile of black
crowned by more black
    front & center in our heads—

    & Voyager 2 winking
    like a gold incisor
    on its way out

of the solar system,
    special record in its belly.

Then there's the *because*
& *I-told-you-so* of it,

the absentee fatherism of it—

    slicking its commissary
goatee with a ringed thumb
    & ringed forefinger

right before a bugged-out
    excuse & non-com grin.

What had happened was . . .

Cassini divisions circling
the East Side again.

Phasers on stun until we're certain.

Almost & *might be* there again,
        the rounded parts of Saturn
        waiting to go green

like the cheap metal under

a Vietnam medal's already
        sketchy plating.

The spacious myth of space, though.
        It's like *this* wide.

Mail-Order Planets

In 1981, Eris's spacious face hadn't been discovered
yet, my mother hadn't taken a day off from Fort Ben
yet, & Pluto was still a planet. One of nine celestial
bodies snapped into drummed orbits around the Sun
like the orthodontic rubber bands no one in Carriage House
had. I hid my gaps by not smiling, imagining an astronaut
future as sharp & fixed as a dentist's smile—236 miles
above Earth where up & down are instructions instead
of directions. Behind a mirrored visor, the singing inside
my American-flagged extravehicular mobility unit
so robust it could keep a black boy from Indiana breathing
in outer space. We didn't have any solar system models
at PS113, so I had to get my own. I dove into dumpsters
searching for cans & bottles under the OJ cartons & maggots
fat in swallows of juice. I dug through frozen dinner boxes
& apple cores shaped like moldy infinities, then foraged
the iced-out underpass—*M&M* ♥ *Kim* painted in moon-
eyed red, then X-ed out with black paint by the time
the frost went away. I hunted the ice- & tire-clogged creek
where I would have spun the bottle with Cynthia
from science class if I wasn't chicken. The A&P paid
by the pound & I dragged sacks stuffed with sand-filled
Schlitz & Tab cans around back where the braceface
sweating on the scale knew my game & paid me anyway.
Three months of collecting & I had enough money

to order our system from the back of a *Star Trek* comic—
all nine planets in adjustable orbits & Earth's majesty
anchoring the third lane. The kid in the ad was as excited
as I was—waiting for the mailman every day after mailing
five wrinkled bills—but the solar system never came.

STARDATE 8107.15

Down in the wrinkled creek,
    with the broken crawdad
claws & heel-crushed
    beer cans. Down in
the creek, below the burnt-
    out house with half
a black wall & part
    of a chimney still hanging
around with Garrett
    & Cynthia & tenacious
mosquitoes buzzing like a radio
    stuck between channels.
I can't come up with enough
    reasons to run back up
to the bridge. Either
    I saw something between
the trees or I saw something
    in the stinking creek. Either
I'm a red shirt or the captain.
    Either I can hear
my mother call or I saw
    a molester peeking from
the drainpipe. Stranger
    danger, but once you stutter,

it doesn't matter. Stranger

    danger & it smells just

like a dumpster down here.

    When it rains, the sewer pipe

dribbles Indianapolis scraps

    right into this creek.

That can't be good

    for the minnows. Fat

gray clouds mean rain?

    My mom is calling me—

I won't hear her down here?

    Those are excuses, probably.

Garrett found an empty beer

    bottle & he's spinning it

on his palm like a propeller.

    He's laughing at me again.

Cynthia found a cracked branch

    spreading like Vulcan fingers

& she's shoe deep in logical

    overflow. It looks like she's

about to call an orchestra

    to attention, but she's slapping

an unfortunate crawdad

    with her knuckled, split stick.

Those Minor Regrets

—after Lynda Hull

We ran around Carriage House East
nonstop like a bunch of nervous mouths—

in jacking-jawing & split orbits—

& the huffing in the throat stack

& double-ply knee cracks as we slid
    Toughskin thick past the dented

    chariots on blocks & lover-graffitied
dumpsters, one after another in industrious,

planetary circuitry. All this disco symmetry,

    this sectioned happenstance
jangling our poked-out vertebrae

& vacant middles & the halogen lights
    shone clearly against

    the chocolate bar as I slipped it
into my pocket at the Village Pantry.

Garrett said, *Man, just take it,* & I did.
　　My first disobedient
accident after my father split.

　　My first calculable maleficence,
guilt now sitting in my center
　　　like the powdered milk

　　everybody drinks sometimes.

Back when I still wanted
　　　to be an astronaut—
　　　in a space shuttle

jetting through stars strobing
　　　as brightly as the front-row
kids we clowned habitually.

　　Right before my nearsightedness
made blurs out of the teacher's
　　　chalk work, extension cords

　　　& raised hands out
　　of branches & leaves.

　　Right above my stomach's

tricky punch, right next to the busted
    harmony of heartbeats

where I sewed a yard-sale
    Star Trek patch thinking

Cynthia might like it.
    Even the front-row kids
made fun of me for that.

    How could I know?
Poor only matters around
    people who aren't poor

& everyone I knew was already
    a trivial thief. Even after

our electric cut off, some needier

neighbor tried to break into
our dark looking for some thing—

just like the sad, redheaded guy

    watching from the same
    Washington Square bench

across from the Flintstones ride
& 25¢ carousel of grinning bunnies

    & horses no one ever rode
    while we waited for the cops
to answer my mother's 911.

After every break-in, to the mall—

safety in the splendor of big cookies
    & pretzel salt, that spinning

disco ball out in Spencer's window

    the closest things to another
    world I can remember.

How to Choose the Next City

On another warm winter day, I'm stuck out
on the court's fringe again like Garrett's mother

was after she tried to run her boyfriend over
while he stretched out near half court. She missed

him but left the Chevy there anyway, idling
& popping until the gas ran out. We all laughed

when her boyfriend rolled out of the way, then
chased after her, apologizing for something.

I'm on the outs again, too—follow-through fingers
hitched below my bottom rib like a name buckle

made out of knuckles. Borrowed ball parked
in my elbow crook & Indianapolis—cracked

backdrop of two, maybe three taller buildings—
unrepentant above the tangles of empty trees where

the older ballers smoked a joint between runs.
My other hand—wrapped around the austere questions

of cities we would move to if only I could grow
& get my jumper right: Cincinnati, Chicago. Almost

Brooklyn, nearly Detroit. Away from Indiana
nearsightedness, away from hooping in slippery

church shoes & getting picked the one after last.
Always next, always stuck on the crest of the court

while the real ballers dribbled & jawed behind
relentless smack talk about busted jumpers, knock-off

shoes, mamas & their respective fatness—all
tangled in sweaty pageantry as glimmering

& sticky as the mall jewelry they borrowed
from each other to shine up for the girls pretending

they weren't watching. A little city of gleaming
gallantry that I was too broke to get a spot in.

Blacks Swinging Low

My black father's absent jurisdiction
    includes this city of skin I'm in.
It includes nickel-plating pinkie rings,

fist-picking Cassinis, one-dropping
    codes in absence of attention. Praying
to go to orbit, in a space shuttle

where everyone looks the same
    in a space suit. From Earth, interstellar
things still look black & white through

a telescope—the Moon, Mars,
    Voyager 2—it doesn't matter. In Indiana,
we got one channel: TV-40, the church

channel. *The Little Rascals* & Stymie's
    meticulously clean-shaven head
as shined up as a Buick handle

when the passenger door shuts: *I wish*
    my pappy was out of jail. I wished
I had some chicken. Then *Leave It*

to Beaver's statutory whiteness cuffed
  between corduroy preachers, one after
another in semicircles. Something happened

between those weekday sermons & I was
  just like the other needy congregants—
lying on my bird-chested bed, peeking

out from behind interlocked hands
  at the rusting coils under the top bunk
curling like black & white galaxies.

Unfunky UFO

The first space shuttle launch got delayed until
Sunday, so we had to watch the shuttle's return
to Earth in class instead—PS113's paunchy black
& white rolled in, the antennae on top adjusted
sideways & down for better reception. That same
day, Garrett stole my new pencil box. That same
day, Cynthia peed her jeans instead of going
to the bathroom & letting Garrett steal her pencil
box. Both of us too upset to answer questions about
space flight, so we got sent to the back of the class.
I smelled like the kind of shame that starts a fight
on a Tuesday afternoon. Cynthia smelled like pee
& everyday Jordache. The shuttle made its slick way
back to Earth, peeling clouds from the monochromatic
sky & we all—even the astronomically marginal—
were winners. American, because a few days before,
a failed songwriter put a bullet in the president
in the name of Jodie Foster. The shuttle looked
like a bullet, only with wings & a cockpit, & when
it finally landed, the class broke into applause
& the teacher snatched a thinning American flag
from the corner, waved it back & forth in honor
of our wounded president & those astronauts.

On this planet   on this planet
      on this mixed-up & American planet
of tin foil shuttles   & hats that still
      tune into disco jams on 106.7 & you
ain't black really   planet. Just kinda
      black because your daddy black planet.
That jive turkey   left you all waiting
      in the living room at the empty window.
Smiling like J.J. Evans   & his Big Mac
      teeth saying *Dyno-mite!* between bites.
& you were King-   Tutting with little arms
      but you never ate a Big Mac. You,
all tan-lined   along your broken afro lines
      on this hungry, yellow kind of planet.

Trumpets Up in Here

—*after* Trumpet *(1984), Jean-Michel Basquiat*

The sprawl & broken crawl on the back
of Basquiat's paints, the thin cleft

of villainous pigments wrapping

each frame like the syntax
in somebody else's relaxed

explanation of lateness: *What had
happened was* . . .

Below blackened crowns,

below words crossed out
as a reminder of what is underneath:

potholes, ashy elbows, & breath

that, in the cold, comes out in red light

& complaint shapes—three lines
from Miles's mouth
in the habit of tardy remunerations.

All of that three-triggered agitation,

all that angry-fingered fruition

like Indianapolis's three-skyscrapered
smile when the sun goes down & even

the colors themselves start talking

  in the same suspicious idiom
  as a brass instrument—

thin throat like a fist,
  flat declinations of pastors
& teachers at Christmas in the inner city.

Shoulders back & heads up when
playing in the holiday choir of hungry

  paints, chins covered
in red scribbles in all of the songs.

Le voyage dans la lune

Since the last break-in,
all of the downstairs windows

    in our townhouse open
as awkwardly as my mouth

in math class:
haphazard tracks bent

    & bent some more
    by screwdrivers

& dithyrambs of fingers
doing their dirty work—

    sometimes in work gloves,
sometimes with galaxies

of fingerprints & nails chewed
    down to the dirty hooks

    underneath. One time
we found a press-on nail

ledged like a glittering smile
where the screen used to be.

The amateur crook kept
    the screen, bronze medal

when she couldn't pry
the window. Things get

    honest with a quickness
after dark, like my mother's borrowed

    Richard Pryor record
    on low: *I used to be really,*

    so poor, I'd walk down
the street . . . you ever

    do that, looking for money
& pretending like you ain't? Every

extra squeak or extra cough:
    a knee to the ribs & from

underneath the crooked
kitchen opening—where

we sometimes hid when
    my mother worked

late, munching on old crackers
from the church bag while

the neighbors got thick
    in their loudness—

next to the burnt-out
stove & through the spaces

    under the curtain's pinned
    hems, we could see

our back neighbors' curtainless
    windows, squares of light

so generous & family filled,
we might have mistaken

them for three motherships
    if they were round.

From the Get-Go Blacks

It hasn't rained in three weeks & my jaw
    is so tight it clicks like my mother's heels
in the early-morning kitchen every time

I try to talk. The sickness thermometer
    in the bathroom drawer is as red as it can
get, but Indy still glistens in the poor people's

time of the year. Every sparkling day wishing
    for its former, cooler self—makeshift
masculinities baby mustached into colorful

spray paints of hustle & grin. Exhaust pipes
    hardly hang on again, scraping light from
potholes unrelentingly, like a refrigerator

door opening in the heat. & later, when
    it gets even hotter, the corrugated need
makes father figures out of delinquent

ballers—quintets of sweaty arms & high
    tops as broken & elbowed as some
other city's name. An air-conditioned

one with deep-ended pools. Whistling
    lifeguards & working water fountains,
even. I'd swim there if I knew how.

STARDATE 8205.01

In the dusty cascade of powdered milk

    mixed with real milk & water to double

in size. In the yeasty hands of home bread

    baking before work to have something

to crumble into open mouths, a couple

    of things on this planet stick to ribs:

fork high hatting an empty bowl,

    bony soup of early-morning sky between

fingers. & we all eat like Christmas Eve

    on payday nights on this planet. We don't

stash bread in drawers or crackers

    under blankets on this planet. We never

hide the mixed milk because it separates

    & spoils too quickly. We don't hide cups

of water because there is plenty to fill

    the evening from its belly to its eyes.

So Far to Go

—*after* St. Joe Louis Surrounded by Snakes *(1982)*,
Jean-Michel Basquiat

In the purplish clutch between evening & more
    evening, boys smoked cigarettes to their minty
ends & talked about *ass like mad hams* & *hips*

like pow, mouths curling with avid adornment
    & vivid hands shaping the air—palms down to palms
up in half circles of perplexity. The C-shapes

the tobacco still glowing between their fingers makes
    is the closest any of them will get to a girl's hip today.
Which is why these courtyard boys, in run-down tanks

& thrifty shirts, cut conversations easily from *Watch*
    how I get at her to *Knuckle up, fool,* throwing shoulders
& fists at each other like minor superheroes without

villains to fight. No capes in bare knuckles. No saving
the block either because every swing breaks something.

Everyone Needs a Chariot

& when that four-wheeled mothership finally
    swings down to carry me home: *Funk not only*
moves, it can remove, you dig? Everyone here

takes the quickest way from curb to door thanks
    to the aspiring villains waiting for their rides.
The blind woman on the right side played

Mothership Connection most late nights in July
    & she knew not to loiter on her way to the stop.
The dealer on the left side sent someone else

to the Village Pantry for Kools the night he let us
    play Atari on the projection TV until after dark.
Everyone should have a marketable skill, the dealer

snorted. Mine started with video games & ended
    someplace in outer space where I could see
without my glasses. The sky was full of blinking

wheels from an arcade game I hadn't played yet
    the first time I was out that late. *Swing down,*
sweet chariot. Stop & let me ride. & below that Thursday

sky: my mother yelling my name from the doorway's
    sunk light, front of her blue housecoat clutched
as tight as the funk George Clinton sang about.

Do Work

—*after* Max Roach *(1984), Jean-Michel Basquiat*

Saturday night—the last blue

of the week & the stars
    were already at work.

& the electricity was still off

    even though my mother
worked at Fort Benjamin Harrison
for the sixth straight day.

& inside our currentless absence,

my first bit of black happenstance,
    the namelessness of it all—

the crass powerlessness of not having.

Our walls didn't even have enough
meat to keep out the drumming.

    We were all cramping
& drinking water & WTLC
    on the portable radio.

Every commercial—
meaty spaghetti & garlic bread

from the Italian spot, chicken
& pie from the bar-stooled diner

next to the Village Pantry.

& I was a drummer,
big-mouthed & without a drumstick,
collecting beats like quick breaths

& belly ache from
being in charge again.

Ascendant Blacks

The power was turned off again the Tuesday morning I got
my curl & Guion S. Bluford became the first black man in outer
space. August 30, 1983. I styled my wet frond like *1999* Prince:
left side tucked behind the ear, dangling mess getting activator
in the same eye I would have used to telescope the *Challenger*
as it flew over Kennedy Space Center in the midnight habit
of black men trying to get out expeditiously. In Indiana, any yellow
brother could be an on-the-fly Prince if he opened his eyes like two
afterburners & hung his lips just a little. Even on the East Side
where we all felt better in groups. Even way over in Pike Township,
where three Pyramids rise as majestically as cranial lumps after
a beat down. Or in Martinsville, a town so precise with its epithets
& buckshot, Bluford wouldn't even fly over it in the daytime.

Beat Boxing

That day the dancers started trying
      to break but somebody broke
the radio while trying to snatch
      a grocery sack from an old lady.
That day the old lady's paper sack
      broke under the weight of absent
expectations & dry spaghetti
      & Granny Smiths fell apart on
the street like busted explanations
      in a British accent: *La Di Da Di,*
we likes to party— That grocery
      mess made Garrett laugh so hard
it built a backbeat. That laugh
      loaned muscle instead of bringing
the knuckle like a side fist beating
      as fat as an apple on a lunchroom
table. A beat that huffed a mad
      circle of knuckle-ups. The rappers
rap when the huff coughs up.
      The breakers break when
this gruff grumble verses up.
      It breathed deep in someone
else's crushing break up & rough
      motives where the handclap

should be. That breathing rim
	shot the whole cluster
of Kangoled knuckleheads. Empty
	grocery sacks between handclaps.
The old lady's wig tilted between
	backslaps & laughs. Out of breath,
that beat rested—a loan shark
	on Thursday prepping for Friday
payday. Nobody breathed as that beat
	made metronomes from breaths.
The old lady went inside to call
	the cops & nobody breathed another
beat as the apple bruised to a stop.

Beat Bop

—after "Beat Bop" (1983), Jean-Michel Basquiat

Carriage House kids see raindrops
    cratering chalk wherever

    one muttering set of beat words
drops its Gs to meet the kneecaps
    of another—

    which leads to mismatched
thought bubbles—

    those humiliating
    & high-strung aphorisms

coalescing above adolescent heads
inked in lightning bolts & stars,

    # signs & questions marks—

chins low, watching sneakers
    squeaking their cursing volume.

& a crown blinking
above it all like a bad streetlamp.
      This lead-in rain—warm up

      to *Friday Night Videos*—

shows us how to sing everything
      except the consonants,
            still grinning like they stole

something, & slim wishbones

& Richard Pryor skits
      snickered in headphones:

& I saw this big-ass
      fist come at me
in slow motion—

I'm talking about
way back from Georgia—

or whatever other R-rated version
of water needs to be beaten out

      of this X-ed out raindrop.

& while we bicep flex
      in parked-car windows,

our tough-guy shufflebucks
& rhyming words go right at each

other in crowded semicircles
    like a right hook's
    muddy knuckles.

Breaking Away

The three knuckles & fingers crowding up to point
back at you are an abacus for all your funky wants.

Hydraulics & multi-pigment supersonics counting it
out at Skateland turned dance floor. Sergio Valente

rocking four parts on the right side where there's no
parking, baby. You need room to get your back up.

You got slow moves like a dump truck backing up.
A stubbed toe trying to get right in the brake light

between sidewalk & trick-legged roboting. You're
just as spunky as a cartoon bomb with a fuse looking

to be lit. Break beats: the struck match & you're blowing
up. Across cutoff sleeves, past rising sun headbands

& American flag wristbands, leg-sweeping every pretty
lady in your imagination before setting the dance line

on stun. Truthfully, you need a bit more activator
for your robot revolutions. You need to chronograph

those windmill intuitions. Your tripped-up moonwalk
is a lot like early service on Sunday. & when you

disco point at the lady in the half-top & biker shorts,
the three fingers pointing back at you join the thumb,

bird-dogging the rhythms of the universe as you orbit
the center of the skate floor like a B Side's stepson.

Boxing Out

I never had hops, so I got on runs
    at Bertha Ross Park the same way
I kept my spot on the community center

squad: immaculately free-throwing
    with follow through, flicked wrist
left hanging for the imaginary game

winner when *winner* meant *fly girlfriend*
    instead of sulking solo in the gym
corner at the community center dance

as the DJ played one slow jam
    on top of another for the unending
couples-only dance. At Bertha Ross,

we collected in our pickup corners
    right in front of a white hard hat
who said, *Gerry Cooney will put*

that big nigger in his place to no one
    in particular while chewing his ham
sandwich down to the red rinds.

We all heard him say it between reverse
        pivots & warm-up jumpers, but acted
like we didn't hear a thing. We didn't

look at each other in the eye, either,
        & still almost won until somebody's
drunk uncle sweating through his Peaches

& Herb shirt called one of those old-
        man fouls. But Cooney didn't beat
Holmes. He didn't even come close.

Map to the Stars

A Schwinn ride away: Eagledale Plaza. Busted shopping
strip of old walkways, crooked parking spaces nicked
like the lines on the sides of somebody's mom-barbered
head. Anchored by the Piccadilly Disco, where a shootout
was guaranteed every weekend—coughing stars shot from
sideways guns shiny enough to light the way for anyone
willing to keep a head up long enough to see. Not me.
I bought the star map shirt for 15¢ at the Value Village
next to the Piccadilly. The shirt was polyester with flyaway
collars, outlined in the forgotten astronomies of disco.
The shirt's washed-out points of light: arranged in horse
& hero shapes & I rocked it in places neither horse nor hero
hung out. Polyester is made from polyethylene & catches
fire easily like wings near a thrift-store sun. Polyethylene,
used in shampoo bottles, gun cases, & those grocery sacks
skidding like upended stars across the parking lot. There
are more kinds of stars in this universe than salt granules
on drive-thru fries. Too many stars, lessening & swelling
with each pedal pump away from the Value Village
as the beaming billboard above spotlights first one DUI
attorney, then another who speaks Spanish so the sky
is constantly chattering, like the biggest disco ball ever.

SOUNDS OF EARTH

Sounds in Sequential Order (Edit)

Music of the Spheres

Frequencies get lean out here, echoing like abandoned ghosts
rattling the forgotten umbrellas & coatless hangers in the front hall
closet. Everyone just ghosted as soon as the summonses came
& the exodus sounded just like the star Jansky didn't mean
to record while he tried to fix the telephone lines. This part
of the sphere doesn't have working phones, so where do we go
next? To rooms of vacant advice & gilded paintings where
the have-it-alls live? To their quadrophonic systems & wood-
cheeked speakers? A golden record in a pulsar map & binary
arithmetic plays 16⅔ RPM while the record changer stacks
requests for traveling music. One LP settling on top of another
LP, a platter of orbits for the rest of the intergalactic voyagers.

Volcanoes, Earthquakes & Thunder

The fact is the Earth doesn't rest.
        It spins & breaks like an LP stepped
on too many times. Polyvinyl chloride
        backing up into itself—rawboned
slopes quaking in elemental underthings
        when nobody is around to pray on it.

All of these migratory people—hymnals
     in hand—who only know the chorus
& want to hear it again & again.

Crickets, Frogs

Chirping, again
     & again

to the stellar back
fence where
     some kind

of under-constellation

     party happens
every night between
May & September.

Stars sequenced
     in various poses
& frogs stretched

     like hungry Xs
close to the pond's
edge. But not close

enough: there's a bridge
     with caution cones

& a newly paved street
in between. & the pond—

twinkling as far
	as the frog eye
can see—is really

a concrete bowl
full of rainwater

in the middle of a future
	office park.

Wild Dog

Domestication only goes as far as the last full
paycheck takes it in these new developments
& barking is an uncertain alarm when there are almost
six houses & one plugged-in streetlamp out here.

Footsteps, Heartbeats, Laughter

One high top after
	the other, the floor

		creaks like a concave chest.

One big, white shoe
in front of the other while
    the beats push

    the sphere's roof up
    to its taller, more
celestial & cogent self.

    One after the other

above the crackups & giggles
    of parent parties

& a refrigerator huffing, so full
of fresh produce & red meat

    the whole, lit sky

sounds like a heart in love—
    pressed into wax,
ready for the next question.

Fire & Speech

A lit match into the abandoned
    house above the creek & the whole
        sky gets as bright as a dashiki

out in the suburbs. All these colors
  scaffolding bricks & the neat perihelions
    of power fists in the air, for this

planet or the next. So many millions
  of miles from the angry human sounds,
    as heavy & magnificent as gravity

pulling on the walled shadow of a man
  in a sideways Pacers cap. He's unarmed.
    Listen to all of the gestures that mean

discontent wherever they are said.
  Listen as leather Africa medallions tangle
    like big noises in a suburban ear.

The First Tools

Headphone to ear, a Radio Shack four-track.
Two borrowed turntables & a duct-taped
microphone: all of this ad-lib circuitry just
waiting for the break beat to open like clouds
over an undiscovered planet. Neither of us
rapped with bass in the voice yet, so DJ Glove
put Richard Pryor's bicentennial questions over
a Mantronix beat to fill in: *We offer this prayer.*

& the prayer is: How long will this bullshit
go on? How long? . . . That is the eternal question!
Man has always asked, How long? Meanwhile,
the crowd that should have been head nodding
shepherds-hooked us off stage in angry brains.

Morse Code

Vernacular of questions
& hooks. Long & short

breaths instead of numbers
or letters. Orbits of digits

in the funky mind
of the wallet & bills balled

up like Tuesday afternoons
in the summer. Oxidizing

the ancients. Harmony
in the mathematic possibilities

of dashes & red blinks
stacked to the stratosphere.

Train, Truck, Tractor, Bus

The morning sky is stacked flat on top of us, like vinyl
waiting its spin on the wheel. The bus stop still smells
like whoever peed in it, even in the upward-looking suburb,
where a tractor keeps ambitious corn in line on the backline
of the polished subdivisions & bulldozers declassify soil
& stubborn tree stumps. Trucks come & go payloaded
with couches & vacation photos & dishes in Bubble Wrap.
The observant, locomotive suburb where the conductor tugs
his train horn, waves back to the children stuck at the crossing
with soggy ice-cream cones & mostly attentive parents.

Mother & Child

The mothership is mostly
    foil with four lights
        unevenly blinking up

top like streetlights about
    to go out. The mothership
        has eight exhaust nozzles

underneath & a funky
    side door with its own
        cascading stair of keyboard

keys underneath ringed
    fingers as it huffs & coughs
        on the swing down to let

us ride. A chorus of drums,
    undeniably on the one.
        A chorus of harmonizing

women, gorgeous as comets,
    & rows & rows of high-
        stepping, glittery stacks

just waiting to get off
    the ship. & the ship
        is the only way any of us

down-&-out blacks are
    going to ease on down
        those future & celestial

roads. Remind both
    mother & child: the whole
        scene pinwheels around

us while we are stuck
    in our tin-foiled
        & ontological patterns.

Life Signs

If EEG patterns
    can show fluctuations

        of thought, then
        thumb & finger

patterns on the piano

        can show changes
of heart—from huddling

        in the bare kitchen
        waiting for Friday

to cooking up deep pots
        of something
with real meat & onions.

        From handclapping
        locks on doors before

        posting the chair up
to roboting in windows

with pristine curtains up
    & a field full
of corn on the other

side of the fence & a service
of stars up above.

    We could take
all of it & nobody
    would notice other

    than the crickets.

A horn tapped politely
    in the distance
    & the mothership hum

waiting to flashlight
    the brain-to-electrode
contraption sketching out

    this whole heartfelt
thing for everyone to see.

Pulsar

Everyone, pick up that skipping record needle
    for future times & future beings. It's elocution,
only with more nomenclature static. We all
    need to put on big sunglasses & cover our ears.
It's a loud, phonetic sound. Neuron on neuron
    sound. It's hyperventilating in the stuck groove
again—word pause word pause static. We all
    need to put on our sunglasses to cover our good
times from these loud habits. We need extra magnetism
    to cover the hurtful ringing in our earringed ears.

STARS ALREADY

Outta Here Blacks

As soon as Mom married Pops:
    off to the suburbs, realm
    of glamorously blue

    swimming pools, carpools

& a spinning rack of comic books
out front at the Village Pantry.

& we were out of Carriage House
like kids as soon as math sub
    turns his back.

    We were out like juice
boxes after lunch.

    We were on the West Side—
nowhere near our old neighborhood—
like a well-organized poverty protest.

No moving truck because
we didn't have anything
    to move out.

    We were so out of there
    I had to dial long distance

to tell Garrett we'd gone.

We were outside our chalk-outlined
     piece of town like a bad pitch.

We were outlying that old spot

     like perfectly spelled
gentrifications. We were as out

of bounds as the *how* & *why*

of black kids with two
     white parents now.

     Desegregation out here.

I got some ice cream out here
like an Eddie Murphy impersonation
     at the watercooler.

     We were as uncomfortable
as a black joke in our air-conditioned

& well-festooned new home.

STARDATE 8705.13

This new planet of once-was farmland, tucked into
    the other side of shiny fences, orbits an eye squint

of skyscrapers & it looks like Indy added a few more
    buildings from this apsis. This new planet of expansion

because that's what you're supposed to do when
    neighbors leave doors unlocked day or night. Big

spaces with no one around, this planet. Garage door
    openers & lights always on, this electrical planet.

Put your hands up high on this planet. Dashboard
    your Gazelles because it's so upbeat, the sunshine

doesn't matter. Everyone is glitzy & aerobic. Bowls
    just for the keys. Bowls just for name-brand cereal.

This planet has storms that pull across the gray sky
    like a duvet, dropping rain & lightning on the necks

of all its citizens & nobody—not giants with mouths
    opened as wide as Geist, not the winged & torch-

carrying angels on the Soldiers & Sailors Monument
    at the center of those distant buildings—can handle

all that electricity coming down. & all the while,
　　pristine Reeboks & spandex & *right foot left foot*

now right from the jazzercise windows down
　　the street on this side of the decorative bridge.

If You're Tired, Then Go Take a Nap

I never liked bridges or cops & there
    are more of both of them in the suburbs,
lording over possibilities like stumbles

do stairs. Down the blue & white set next
    to the small gym after first period, shoelace
caught under a new bully's foot. He would

have gotten stole on in Carriage House, but
    not by me. Gots to chill or it'll get worse:
in blue Jams & pushed off summer's slick

ledge, long fall into the private pool broken
    into three distinct verses: the flail & giggling
girls, the sun-stroked lifeguard's exclamation,

& the red-handed water's backslap rising up,
splitting into two, more chlorinated skies.

Intergalactic Blacks

Guion S. Bluford
doesn't fit into the astronaut
tradition any more

than the A Side
of *Sounds of Earth*—

gilded in the second spinning

Voyager space probe—
parlays the real ruckus

we make in our earthen
hustle of engine contrition—

nigger used as noun & adjective
again in NASA hallways.

Sounds is beautiful, though,
with its thin skin of golden language.

Where to begin? Where is
the smiling redress
of planets?

Where are those intergalactic
    Star Wars spaces
    without races?

Hello. What have we here?
says Lando Calrissian
from his cloud city.

    & he's not even
in the astronaut team portrait—

    Solo Brother Bluford
    in his colonel outfit,

Soul Brother No. 1—

    ringed in whiteness
like the loneliest dot on a die.

Record Changer

To the left of the neighbors' barbeque, variations
of the same house ringed by the same foliage—
adolescent bushes, their green tufts of low-lying sky.
Dads, red faced & bearded, in back someplace,
turning pure meat over hot coals. The record
player is inside, wood-boxed speakers propped
in the windows. To the right, across the still-seeded
yard, our two-story just as square & impeccable
as the rest. We want Prince but *Rumours* keeps
restarting itself: *Now here you go again, you say.*
One neighbor asks, *Now, where did you come from
again?* & we say, *California, like Fleetwood Mac.*
& nobody asks anything else. & because nobody
hunts for dinner in the suburbs, we put down
our implements of half step & appetite, sidestep
the moon as it descends into a whole plateful
of charred thighs & wings. We collectivize
the back-in-the-days way as tenaciously as chicken
legs undress themselves at a cul-de-sac party, then
raise the stripped bones to history. Out here, there
isn't any, so history is whatever we want it to be.

Strange Celestial Roads

There's a father sleeping it off in every master bedroom
    of the cul-de-sac the morning after, so Saturday
morning is a snooze. The moon is still out, eyeballing
    the quiet street like Sun Ra did his Arkestra. Somebody
has to be the father figure for all of those musical notes.
    No school buses to huff after, no mothers yelling
their children onward. The only weekend noise is us,
    kicking rocks—so bored we can't even hear each other—
on a celestial swirl of asphalt that will be a playground
    one day. We stand, right feet extended in unison
like foos men, rock after rock arcing at sorry angles
    toward the open bar that hopes to dangle four swings.
Some rocks go through, some miss as we balance
    on concrete meant to backstop hopscotch & echo
knock knock jokes. Not somebody's father yelling, *You got
    to be kidding me,* after he opens the property tax bill.
These bars were placed here for some other, future kids
    to be dragged from by big ears or hair-matted necks
back to the unavoidable arguments, fist-to-face noises,
    & the sweet, bleating saxophones that come next.

Space Is the Place

I would rather be back in Carriage House
    stashing away stale bread

than in this abundance of landscaped dirt
    where the neighbors' dog-walk

greetings are twice as loud
    as their arguments.

    All those unworn sneakers
    parked in shoe boxes
    & stacked on each other

in my brand-new closet,

just waiting for me to wear out
the ones I'm wearing now.

    & a path to the fence
lined with muddy sneaker & paw prints.

Sedentary earthmovers of various
sizes waiting for things to dry

to finish the new neighborhood
    playground or more houses

& water pooling below
　　the high-angled driveway

as distracting as the newly named
cul-de-sac. & from the garage

windows—busted
　　wheels of light coming
　　from the other houses.

*

But thanks for the protracted quiet
　　of three-wheeled moons

　　　　out here. Thanks for the speckled
　　　　memory of a glimmering sink

& new counters & the cuticle of sawdust
　　in one kitchen corner out here.

New, white stepdad. Nothing off-brand.

My gut, finally high-stepping
　　& rounding celestially
like the whole day was a buffet.

One bedroom for each of us.

A window with crisp blinds in each room
looking out over our gated & future yards.

*

Now your future is unwound mid-stride
like the windup robot Garrett swiped
from A&P. Now, you're ghosting between
breaths—a knobby runner's serenade
to the sad ribbon of pavement at the end
of the street, flat feet & knees creaking—
the dirt mounds that will one day sprout
houses under the snowflakes of developmental
embellishment. You keep running—through
the remaining woods, past the farmer's field
hibernating on the other side of the trees
on the right. No hyphenated gunshots yet.
No high school band robberies or hammer
assaults yet. Rabbits & hungry squirrels watch
you run by. No needy neighbors. Just stumps
& bulldozers waiting for future opportunities
in the snow. All of this dirt came from some
other dirt repeating itself & you stand on top
of its frozen remains, arms raised like the Y
in YMCA. Look at you now. You are high-fiving
yourself in the middle of a future strip mall.

Sold to the Man with the Mouth

Even in the suburban center
    of mall-bought telescopes

& bedsheet ladders, unsubsidized
    father figures collaborate
in embouchure shapes to offer

a whole lot of bad advice.
    Their split-pin maxims

& Reagan fist-shaking axioms

& walls coming down while
the women around are old adages

    scuttled like empty
tall boys tossed on the side
of newly plowed roads without

    a car in sight.
Afterward, somebody chuckles
    through the wall

like a housebound blue jay.

Others, mothers & sons,
  watch from their angles
  of disappointment, hoping

their particular father is pulling
  into the driveway
  after his late meeting

or trip to the grocery

  or head-clearing cigarette
that somehow took him
all the way to Chattanooga:

Trying to get this money right
  for you & no one
  believes him—not the son

practicing his macho in the mirror,

  not the mustached mouth
that exhaled a neighborhood of words
  to begin with. Not

  the mother blinking
at the brand-new receiver
  like a tired astronomer.

STARDATE 8705.29

The Monday the new neighbor boy
    asked me to say he was with us
at St. Luke's Sunday service was the same
    day this family planet began folding
in on itself. All of the bowling league
    neighbors stowed balls in the bottoms
of marbled closets. All of the barbeque
    neighbors packed up their Fleetwood
Mac & meat thermometers, redirected
    their gossip currency & knew: getting
away from the blacks like this one—
    this one who took a gun & a hammer
to the assistant band teacher—is exactly
    why they'd selected segmented floor
plans & vinyl siding out here to begin with.
    They said the band teacher dragged
himself almost a mile through the locked
    school to a pay phone to call 911.
They said the neighbor boy was snipping
    off his fingerprints with nail clippers
in the back of Geography when the cops
    arrested him. & the floral curtains
came down & the garage doors snapped
    shut like the neighbors' mouths anytime

we walked by & tall gates went up around
    the planet almost as quickly as For Sale
signs showed up while the moving trucks
    monotonously came & went from
the cul-de-sac like industrious detectives.

Business as Usual

After the hammer assault & the move-outs,
nobody left in the cul-de-sac cared when
we sported Kangols bent down over our ears
like big-headed church bells. I had one eye
squeezed so tight it looked like the turbo dial
on a bag phone. The other eye pressed into
a paper towel tube like a thrift-store telescope.
The whole sky: as astronomical as the goatee
I couldn't grow back when we first moved
to Pike. No more astronaut aspirations,
but things are looking sky-high in the eyebrow-
smoothing absolution of acne cream & Genera
sweatshirts, sleeves pushed up to my elbows.
A gold earring in each ear winking like pirates.
The whole time, my homeboy Eric tried
for second base in the back of the family minivan
parked in between For Sale signs: *All the ladies
love E, the green-eyed bandit.* The heartsick seats
& bubbled privacy tint, his slapped face, van door
smashed shut like EPMD beats. I sat on our porch
with my Walkman clicked on, adding up lightning
bugs like numbers on a phone pad. 8 - 9 - * - 1 - 4
still plays the *Close Encounters of the Third Kind*
theme. & later, the minivan's moon roof pushed up
on the ride out to Eagle Creek where Preludes

& Tauruses with five stars bump endless cassettes
of criminal threats: *When I roll I stroll, cool always
pack a tool.* Eric's face still hurt from the slap
as minnows in their industrious gangs nibbled
skinny-dipping rib cages & pale ankles near
the reservoir bottom. Their glossy gills opening
like fingers stumbling to make the gang signs
we suburban boys probably saw on MTV.

Crossover Blacks

It probably sounds like a sneaker
catching on clean hardwood,
    but it's the plutoid

of expectations annoyed by
    its small circumference—

enough gerrymandered rock
    left to crack the jaw
    of any brother who can't

    play ball. The pretend
    planet orbits him—
across parking lots & into

bagel shops—like a rain cloud
    in a cartoon.

Dude, you play ball, right?

The whole thing sounds
like a rocket ship
    cresting the perfect moon

of a white girlfriend's
    explanation to her parents.

Him & his slick silhouette
while his boys watch him toss out
brick after brick after brick

like tokens spent at the State Fair.

Pass the rock, dude.

Him & his pack
   of white friends—

      a flotilla of jumpers
   & pale layups & we're all

         rising up in the gospel
         of headbands & Chuck Taylors

Tuesday afternoons at the Y.

Dude. Pass the rock.

In Indiana, you either play
      ball or deal with abjection

everywhere like a rocket ship
crashed into the moon's eye.

I Remember When I Met U, Baby

—for Prince Rogers Nelson (1958–2016)

Prince is everywhere in his own head.
Prince is everywhere, but here instead—
lipstick & purple eyeliner smudging
every gyrating phonograph & magnificently
heeled ankle in this pre-matrimonial scene
like regrettable graffiti. Prince's B Sides
cut into the splits, then smooths both
eyebrows staring right at the other B Sides
like the daddy of a shotgun bride. Prince's
side-buttoned satisfaction, his actionable
purpleness all wrapped up in lace is the best
exit for an *I'll-call-you-sometime* morning.
Prince won't call because he doesn't have
a phone. Prince, all alone, is more disco
vision than lace premonition in 1981—
motorcycling by some star-pocked lake that
ain't Minnetonka on his way to the studio.
Gigolo of frozen breath & breasts by every
icebound body of water that glimmers
like a dance floor turned on for passersby
to see. & breath: in out, in out, in out on
the downbeat until it's a trochaic turn-on.
Prince wears his makeup to bed so his face

is always on. Underneath, Prince is light
skinned & Midwest where one yellow is just
as bright as the next. His falsettoing fingers,
fancy hair, magnanimous tongue & baby,
they were all stars there in their thigh-highs
& finery. Prince is already there before
he gets there—Minneapolis or Indianapolis
where every yellow boy knows a Jheri curl
can make him a close-enough Prince after
10pm. Prince counts to 10 starting at 10
& the montage begins: motorcycle rides
to a thumping after party where the ladies
& men in his purple circle believe in ruffled
gestures like *I'm just a virgin & I'm on*
my way to be wed. That's when two purple
doors push open into a steamy bathtub
of surprise. That's when there's an impossibly
deep Prince breath & then—

New Developments

Smiles make surprises out of every reddening face.
More neighborly, too, in the time when no one

talks to us: every combed-over & calligraphed
father, shorts pulled up for whatever reason fathers

hike up that high. There are six different colors
of black in calligraphy, but the only black north

of 56th Street is us. We keep moving further out
& the universe keeps opening up more itinerant

moons & galaxies. Nothing like a rocket in the eye
to make suburban moons criminal: *Sorry. Didn't*

recognize you in that sweatshirt. Nothing like new
guard dogs barking after hours to wake the formerly

aspiring astronaut. *Now this is living,* the dad says,
standing on the front step next to his dogs, fallen

leaves loitering along the insistently demarcated
property lines. Fences & more fences blocking off

bits of land below the expanding sky map while
the rest of the roundabout worlds try to keep up.

Basketball feat. Galileo & EPMD

I split every bit of sunlight at College Park's ball court—land
    of sweaty Reebok tees & patriotic wristbands—escalating
to the rim like every player on that court would do

to the Lafayette Square Mall mezzanine on the weekends. Every
    bit of tangled shine around my neck: a hypotenuse of intention.
Highlights are the only lights in my low-rise space of sneaker

to shin & elbow to crown. The only time I dunked, the court
    exploded like a party hearing "You Gots to Chill" for the first
time. & when the smoke cleared, I hung as tight as a sweaty

headband on that rim, talking smack to the other nine ballers
    & to their nine mamas. Then the slipping & cracking. Then
two months left-handing jumpers, one-handing prom photos,

smudged scribbles on my cast, while the basketball rotated
as insistently as the back-spinning apple that split Galileo's wig.

Illinois Abe Lincoln's Hat

blacks painted onto bricks & split vinyl on the East Side,
jaws as tight as window locks with the curtains drawn
& behind that diligent fabric: blacks already tucked
into homemade forts—folding chairs, wobbly backbones
& the whole, snowy world waiting outside like ghost
stories whispered around the last sputtering match. & later,
top sheets pulled up over heads from fear of mirrors
at midnight or some backfired beater's rusty pop pop pop
after the key twists at the edge of the week. No doubt:
Tuesday is the scariest day in Section 8, but Friday is right
after it in the suburbs. & after those trembling weekdays,
even more blacks with money disappearing & reappearing
as unexpectedly as poltergeists inside of TVs & haunted
trees with fast fingers in West Side yards. & still not
a wavelength of any kind for a black to put in the bank.
The inks in everybody's hatted & contracting checkbooks
don't change black. Some front-row architecture might.
Some guns, too, & their loud, colorful opportunities:
whatever version of black is inside a fist around a grip.
Not a color, really—more like the face a man makes in
the glinting face of a gun pointed at him every single day.

Welcome Back to Earth

—after Yusef Komunyakaa

& these Indiana stars spill

like Pops's generous nightcap.

These stars glint
like a doorknob in a night-light.

Stars squinting like somebody's uncle
shooting set shots in College Park.

Midday heat. There's
history in that warm

backspin. Two stars—a sideways
wink. There's history in that again.

The Pacers never contend.

The shimmering substances
of Reggie Miller & them:
layups, fast breaks.

Stars always got explaining to do,
like the fall day I Schwinned all

the way to College Park
to see my girl without permission

at the same time Pops left
the grocery. We passed each other

at the 86th Street intersection
& he chased me down

at least two other streets
      & across the basketball court

in his white minivan
      before I gave in.

I mean, he drove *onto*
the basketball court & I had

to give in. He said, *What*
      is this star shit?

Every humiliating moment
of minivan tire on free throw
      line is starish. Belt dangling

like follow through after a three
      & it's clean. A gold buckle

shining on the downswing.

    That singing sound?

That's the sonics of a failed suburb

lotioning its post-game frown.

Antique Blacks

The antique blacks
belong to me.
—Sun Ra

The sonic singing
of Jansky's star noises—

up & down like horns
in a chorus,

rapturously rewinding feedback

the way a crown of stars would
if crowns were stars for anyone

other than Sun Ra—

13 of them clustered around his elbows
& ears & the hardworking tape deck

circling itself like a brass heliosphere
when he said:

My story is not part of history.
Because history repeats itself.

But my story is endless—
it never repeats itself.

One hand fingering an allegory
of astronaut & ancient prototype
        on the fat piano bench

in Auntie's front room back
on the East Side with plastic-

covered furniture. We don't call
        her "Auntie," really,

        because she was blind.
Her phonograph spins jazz
most of the time—

        right down the street
from a pool hall ringed by posters

        for DJ throw-downs
& Under-21 battles of the bands.

All of that razzmatazz, cluttered

side tables & decorative lamps—

how did she get around them?—

the closest we'll get
to explorers & outer space.

Crickets, Racists

Voyager 2's golden record
spun someplace in the space

between Uranus & Neptune
    the night I pedaled

    my new 10-speed
along Georgetown Road's

unfinished edge & the Datsun
    driver necked out

of the passenger window:
    Off the road, nigger!

His mouth—cracked
& full of open teeth—

right there, screaming
    in my face like Coach

yelling one more thing about
Bobby Knight during line laps.

    & then I was in a ditch—
front wheel bent like a surprise,

as useless as half a moon.
Sitting there, in the cricketed

grass, I heard some
of the same sounds of Earth—

etched in copper & plated
in gold for the long ride out

into a city of comets—
spinning so unrelentingly

I kept losing parts
between exhales.

Emily Dickinson feat. Basketball & EPMD

I read poetry out here, spinning the spindles of happenstance—
    its em dashery like the closed eye of a winking man
used for a record needle. I love when the laces of my suede

kicks come undone like the best-laid plans. & when I crouch
    to tie those boys up, I love savoring the shy glory of my girl's
skirted knee. Her stitched hem branching like the feathered

stems in a blue boa she would never wear. There are too
    many boas in this world & the first feather in their garish
elegance: America, home of lovers & EPMD breaking

car speakers like high school curfews since 1988 someplace
    where I loved summer, the dash from one hoop to the other,
a stray kitten, off balance & chewing a moth in the bleachers

before we fed him a hamburger & somebody's *Business
as Usual* cassette untangling bit by bit like laughs.

If there was ever a chance to go to outer space,

  it wasn't here & it wasn't for me, as off balance

on this distant planet as a buster getting a mouthful

  of knuckles. If there was a possibility of making it

out of this heliosphere, there never really was here.

  Four eyes giggling at me like a laugh track. Black

skin, you can't win in the space race no matter

  what Sun Ra says. Everyone except him agreeing

on these facts like a laugh track. Looking up through

  the round circumstance of a basketball hoop from

a suburb of amateur astronauts. Looking up from this

  corner of black constriction & wind knocked out

of words. This cricket-ticking suburb of fanciful

  neighbors & their distant, but unrelenting chatter.

Code-Switching Blacks

All lowercase things in here, all spacing

things in here & those words—

    & that vernacular hubbub—

    & that code switch tripping

on curbs in triplicate—
      three fingers on black & white keys,
      three huffed-up blacks on the upswing

of Indianapolis's West Side. Words work

the fast magic like a magician's
fingers fanned out as a W—

    tingling fingers over here, white
chickens pecking the rain's thin wrist

    over there—
    building a nest egg

on every great crescendo
    of winged g-dropping.

After the Stars

are more winged galaxies, parading
    like fresh teenagers in the middle
of the mall & everyone is watching.

Past the food court: a crisp parking
    lot, Little Eagle Creek, slender
between the neon shops & packed

Cineplex. After that, three street
    lights bird-squawking our subdivision—
its baby trees & covered wagon

mailboxes going no place fast
    in turnaround ruts. There are more
undiscovered planets out there

than names to use on them
    & I won't get to step on any one
other than this one. The sky still

looks different west of the shuffling
    have-nots—all of these decorative
planters & refrigerator magnets

& every night gleams like payday
  back in Carriage House. One time
I rode my new 10-speed hands-free

past the Overland Court sign where
  pavement breaks into gravel & dirt
at the undeveloped edge. I almost

made it to the aspiring houses
  at the end of their lead-ins marked
with yellow-ribboned stakes

& muddy amalgamations before
  I lost balance looking up. Upward
mobility equals stars in every

thing: the neighbors who moved
  out into even further orbits—
Zionsville, Carmel, new fields

& streets waiting for names.
  The neighbors who couldn't move,
stoic on porches like resilient

pieces of a constellation. One
  black sky above them all. Pop's
minivan & its forever stuck left

signal ticking like a probe's beacon

    as the brake lights on the way out

of the cul-de-sac redden mulch & rocks,

the upstarting yews & their split wigs

    of foliage. One sedan per driveway

& one tree centering each & every yard.

Collectable Blacks

This is the g-dropping vernacular
    I am stuck in. This is the polyphone
where my head is an agrarian gang
    sign pointing like a percussion mallet
to a corn maze in one of the smaller
    Indiana suburbs where there aren't
supposed to be black folks. Be cool & try
    to grin it off. Be cool & try to lean
it off. Find a kind of black & bet on it.
    I'm grinning to this vernacular
like the big drum laugh tracks a patriotic
    marching band. Be cool & try to ride
the beat the same way me, Pryor,
    & Ra did driving across the 30th Street
Bridge, laughing at these two dudes
    with big afros like it's 1981 peeing into
the water & looking at the stars. Right
    before Officer Friendly hit his lights.
Face the car, fingers locked behind
    your heads. Right after the fireworks
started popping off. *Do I need to call*
    the drug dog? Right after the rattling
windows, mosquitoes as busy in my ears
    as 4th of July traffic cops. Right before

the thrill of real planets & pretend planets
  spun high into the sky, Ra throwing up
three West Side fingers, each ringed
  by pyrotechnic glory & the misnomer
of the three of us eyeballing the cop's
  club as it swings down at the exact same
time Pryor says, *Cops put a hurting on your*
  ass, man. & fireworks light up in the same
colors as angry knuckles if you don't
  duck on the double. Especially on the West
Side—more carnivorous than almost any
  other part of Earth Voyager 2 saw when
it snapped a blue picture on its way out
  of this violently Technicolor heliosphere.

NOTES

The Blacks cycle in this book is dedicated to Guion S. Bluford, Richard Pryor, Sun Ra, and the thirteen other black astronauts who have made it to outer space so far.

"Final Frontier" is inspired by Gwendolyn Brooks's poem "The Explorer."

"Those Minor Regrets" is inspired by Lynda Hull's poem "Midnight Reports."

"Blacks Swinging Low" includes dialogue from Stymie in the *Our Gang* short "A Lad an' a Lamp" (1932).

"Le voyage dans la lune" includes a quote from Richard Pryor's "I Hope I'm Funny," from *That Nigger's Crazy* (Reprise, 1975).

"Everyone Needs a Chariot" includes a verse from Parliament's "Mothership Connection" from *Mothership Connection* (Casablanca Records, 1975).

"Beat Boxing" is dedicated to my rapping partner in 1985–86, Ché Townsend, aka C-Lux. The poem includes one of Slick Rick's verses from "La Di Da Di" (Reality Records, 1984).

"Beat Bop" includes part of Richard Pryor's skit "Keeping in Shape," from *Wanted: Live in Concert* (Warner, 1978).

"Sounds in Sequential Order (Edit)" is based on Ann Druyan's selection and arrangement of nineteen categories of sounds for the *Sounds of Earth* record in the Voyager space probes. A detailed explanation of Druyan's process can be found in *Murmurs of Earth* (Random House, 1978). "The First Tools" section of the poem includes a quote from Richard Pryor's "Bicentennial Prayer," from *Bicentennial Nigger* (Warner, 1976).

"If You're Tired, Then Go Take a Nap": The title is an EPMD verse from "You Gots to Chill," from *Strictly Business* (Fresh Records, 1988).

"Record Changer" includes a verse from "Dreams" by Fleetwood Mac, from *Rumours* (Warner, 1977).

"*I Remember When I Met U, Baby*": The title is a verse from "Head" by Prince from his album *Dirty Mind* (Warner, 1981).

"Illinois Abe Lincoln's Hat": The title is one of sixteen different names Crayola has given to the black crayon.

"Welcome Back to Earth" was inspired by Yusef Komunyakaa's poems "More Girl Than Boy" and "Slam, Dunk, & Hook."

The phrase "antique blacks" is from a Sun Ra poem performed in a 1974 concert and is featured on his album *Antique Blacks* (El Saturn Records, 1978). The poem also includes a quote from Sun Ra in the documentary *A Joyful Noise* (1980).

"Collectable Blacks" includes a quote from Richard Pryor's skit "Niggers vs. Police," from *That Nigger's Crazy* (Reprise, 1975).

ACKNOWLEDGMENTS

My thanks to the editors and staffs of the magazines and journals in which these poems have appeared, often with different titles and in different versions:

American Poetry Review: "Adds Up to Something," "Beat Down," "Do Work," "Illinois Abe Lincoln's Hat," "Outta Here Blacks," "So Far to Go," "Sold to the Man with the Mouth"

Barely South Review: "Crickets, Racists"

Boulevard: "Everyone Needs a Chariot"

Copper Nickel: "Breaking Away," as "The Antique Blacks": "Antique Blacks," "Ascendant Blacks," "Blacks Swinging Low," "Code Switching Blacks," "Collectable Blacks," "Crossover Blacks," "Intergalactic Blacks," "Post-Vietnam Blacks," "Star Struck Blacks"

Gulf Coast: "From the Get Go Blacks," "Those Minor Regrets," "Unfunky UFO"

Hobart: "I Remember When I Met U, Baby"

The Louisville Review: "Mail-Order Planets"

Miami Rail Magazine: "If You're Tired, Then Go Take a Nap," "Welcome Back to Earth"

the minnesota review: "& Later," "Basketball feat. Galileo & EPMD," "Emily Dickinson feat. Basketball & EPMD," "Final Frontier"

Platte Valley Review: "Record Changer"

Poetry: "Map to the Stars"

Prairie Schooner: "Boxing Out"

The Rumpus: "Business as Usual"

Southern Indiana Review: "After the Stars," "STARDATE 8705.13," "STARDATE 8809.22"

Spoon River Poetry Review: "New Developments"

TriQuarterly: "How to Choose the Next City," *"Le voyage dans la lune"*
Union Station: "Space Is the Place"
"Read Between the Lines" (November 22, 2013), "Trumpets Up in Here,"
    (September 4, 2015), and "Strange Celestial Roads" (September 9,
    2016) were featured in the *Poem-A-Day* series from the Academy of
    American Poets (www.poets.org).
"Unfunky UFO" appears in the anthologies *The New Census: An Anthol-
    ogy of Contemporary American Poetry* (Rescue Press, 2014) and *New
    Poetry from Midwest* (New American Press, 2015).
"Beat Boxing" and "Breaking Away" appear in *The Breakbeat Poets: New
    American Poetry in the Age of Hip Hop* (Haymarket Books, 2015).
"Those Minor Regrets" (December 15, 2015) was featured on Poetry
    Daily (www.poems.com).
"Emily Dickinson feat. Basketball & EPMD," "Map to the Stars," and
    "Crickets, Racists" appear in *Read America(s): An Anthology* (Locked
    Horn Press, 2016).
"& Later," "Final Frontier," and "Sold to the Man with the Mouth"
    appear in *Revise the Psalm: Work Celebrating the Writing of Gwendolyn
    Brooks* (Curbside Splendor, 2017).

Deepest thanks to the friends and family who helped make this collection
possible, each in incomparable ways: Erin Belieu, Sherwin Bitsui, Catherine
Bowman, Melba Joyce Boyd, Joan Brown, Gabrielle Calvocoressi, Allison
Hedge Coke, P. Scott Cunningham, Oliver de la Paz, Ross Gay, Terrance
Hayes, Richard Johnson, Rodney Jones, A. Van Jordan, Melanie Jordan,
Allison Joseph, Ruth Ellen Kocher, Quraysh Ali Lansana, Shara McCal-
lum, Kevin Neireiter, Cedric Ross, Sean Singer, and Jon Tribble.

Gratitude to the John Simon Guggenheim Memorial Foundation, the
Lannan Foundation, the Office of the Vice Provost for Research at Indiana
University Bloomington, the Poetry Center at the University of Arizona, and
United States Artists for their generous support while I worked on this book.

Many thanks to my editor, Paul Slovak, for his insight and for help-
ing me to shape this project.

Lastly, thank you to Stacey and Marley for giving me a big enough
boost to see over the cornfields.

Stephen Sproull

Adrian Matejka is the author of *The Big Smoke* (Penguin, 2013), which was a winner of the Anisfield-Wolf Book Award and finalist for the National Book Award and the Pulitzer Prize. His other books are *Mixology* (Penguin, 2009), which was selected for the National Poetry Series, and *The Devil's Garden* (Alice James Books, 2003), winner of the New York/New England Award. Among his other honors are a Guggenheim Fellowship, a Lannan Literary Fellowship, and a Simon Fellowship from United States Artists. He lives with his family in Bloomington, Indiana.

JOHN ASHBERY
Selected Poems
Self-Portrait in a Convex Mirror

PAUL BEATTY
Joker, Joker, Deuce

JOSHUA BENNETT
The Sobbing School

TED BERRIGAN
The Sonnets

LAUREN BERRY
The Lifting Dress

PHILIP BOOTH
Lifelines: Selected Poems 1950–1999

JULIANNE BUCHSBAUM
The Apothecary's Heir

JIM CARROLL
Fear of Dreaming: The Selected Poems
Living at the Movies
Void of Course

ALISON HAWTHORNE DEMING
Genius Loci
Rope
Stairway to Heaven

CARL DENNIS
Another Reason
Callings
New and Selected Poems 1974–2004
Practical Gods
Ranking the Wishes
Unknown Friends

DIANE DI PRIMA
Loba

STUART DISCHELL
Dig Safe

STEPHEN DOBYNS
Velocities: New and Selected Poems: 1966–1992

EDWARD DORN
Way More West

ROGER FANNING
The Middle Ages

ADAM FOULDS
The Broken Word

CARRIE FOUNTAIN
Burn Lake
Instant Winner

AMY GERSTLER
Crown of Weeds
Dearest Creature
Ghost Girl
Medicine
Nerve Storm
Scattered at Sea

EUGENE GLORIA
Drivers at the Short-Time Motel
Hoodlum Birds
My Favorite Warlord

DEBORA GREGER
By Herself
Desert Fathers, Uranium Daughters
God
Men, Women, and Ghosts
Western Art

TERRANCE HAYES
Hip Logic
How to Be Drawn
Lighthead
Wind in a Box

NATHAN HOKS
The Narrow Circle

ROBERT HUNTER
Sentinel and Other Poems

MARY KARR
Viper Rum

JACK KEROUAC
Book of Blues
Book of Haikus
Book of Sketches

JOANNA KLINK
Circadian
Excerpts from a Secret Prophecy
Raptus

JOANNE KYGER
As Ever: Selected Poems

ANN LAUTERBACH
Hum
If in Time: Selected Poems, 1975–2000
On a Stair
Or to Begin Again
Under the Sign

CORINNE LEE
Plenty

PHILLIS LEVIN
May Day
Mercury
Mr. Memory & Other Poems

PATRICIA LOCKWOOD
Motherland Fatherland Homelandsexuals

WILLIAM LOGAN
Macbeth in Venice
Madame X
Strange Flesh
The Whispering Gallery

ADRIAN MATEJKA
The Big Smoke
Map to the Stars
Mixology

MICHAEL MCCLURE
Huge Dreams: San Francisco and Beat Poems

ROSE MCLARNEY
Its Day Being Gone

DAVID MELTZER
David's Copy: The Selected Poems of David Meltzer

ROBERT MORGAN
Dark Energy
Terroir

CAROL MUSKE-DUKES
An Octave above Thunder
Red Trousseau
Twin Cities

ALICE NOTLEY
Certain Magical Acts
Culture of One
The Descent of Alette
Disobedience
In the Pines
Mysteries of Small Houses

WILLIE PERDOMO
The Essential Hits of Shorty Bon Bon

LIA PURPURA
It Shouldn't Have Been Beautiful

LAWRENCE RAAB
The History of Forgetting
Visible Signs: New and Selected Poems

BARBARA RAS
The Last Skin
One Hidden Stuff

MICHAEL ROBBINS
Alien vs. Predator
The Second Sex

PATTIANN ROGERS
Generations
Holy Heathen Rhapsody
Wayfare

ROBYN SCHIFF
A Woman of Property

WILLIAM STOBB
Absentia
Nervous Systems

TRYFON TOLIDES
An Almost Pure Empty Walking

SARAH VAP
Viability

ANNE WALDMAN
Gossamurmur
Kill or Cure
Manatee/Humanity
Structure of the World Compared to a Bubble

JAMES WELCH
Riding the Earthboy 40

PHILIP WHALEN
Overtime: Selected Poems

ROBERT WRIGLEY
Anatomy of Melancholy and Other Poems
Beautiful Country
Box
Earthly Meditations: New and Selected Poems
Lives of the Animals
Reign of Snakes

MARK YAKICH
The Importance of Peeling Potatoes in Ukraine
Unrelated Individuals Forming a Group Waiting to Cross